ROSES

ROSES

An Illustrated Treasury
Compiled by Michelle Lovric

COURAGE
BOOKS

an imprint of
RUNNING PRESS
Philadelphia • London

Canadian representatives: General Publishing Co., Ltd., 30 Lesmill
Road, Don Mills, Ontario M3B 2T6.

9 8 7 6 5 4 3 2 1
Digit on the right indicates the number of this printing.

Library of Congress Cataloging-in-Publication Number 94–72603

ISBN 1–56138–550–6

Cover design by Toby Schmidt
Interior design by Frances J. Soo Ping Chow
Edited by Brian Perrin
Typography by Justin T. Scott

Published by Courage Books, an imprint of
Running Press Book Publishers
125 South Twenty-second Street
Philadelphia, Pennsylvania 19103–4399

The author gratefully acknowledges the permission of the following
to reproduce copyrighted material in this book:

P. 18: From "The Rose," from *The Collected Poems of Theodore Roethke*.
Copyright © 1963 by Beatrice Roethke, Administratrix of the
Estate of Theodore Roethke. By permission of Doubleday, a divi-
sion of Bantam Doubleday Dell Publishing Group, Inc., in the
U.S.A. and Canada, and by permission of Faber and Faber Ltd. in
the U.K. and Commonwealth.

P. 19: "Roses" from *The Complete Poems of D. H. Lawrence*, edited by
V. de Sola Pinto and F. W. Roberts. Copyright © 1964, 1971
Angelo Ravagli and C. M. Weekley, Executors of the estate of
Frieda Lawrence Ravagli. By permission of Viking Penguin, a
division of Penguin Books U.S.A., Inc., and by permission of
Laurence Pollinger Ltd.

P. 39: From "somewhere i have never travelled, gladly beyond,"
from *Complete Poems, 1904–1962* by e. e. cummings, edited by
George J. Firmage. By permission of Liveright Publishing
Corporation in the U.S.A. and Canada, and by permission of W. W.
Norton & Company in the U.K. and Commonwealth. Copyright ©
1931, 1959, 1979, 1991 the Trustees for the e. e. cummings trust.

P. 43: From "Sonnet on the Death of the Man Who Invented Plastic
Roses," from *Liquid Paper* by Peter Meinke. Copyright © 1991 Peter
Meinke. By permission of the University of Pittsburgh Press.

P. 44: "Dying Roses" from *Dark Roses* by Michael Bullock, first published by Third Eye, London, Canada. Copyright © 1994 Michael
Bullock.

INTRODUCTION

THE ROOTS OF THE ROSE EXTEND FAR BACK INTO HISTORY. IN ALL PLACES, IN ALL TIMES, IT HAS BEEN THE VIVID, SWEET-SCENTED SYMBOL OF FRAGILE BEAUTY, PURE, DIVINE LOVE, AND PASSIONATE DESIRE. IT PERSONIFIES ALL FLOWERS AND ALL FRAGRANCE, JUST AS IT EPITOMIZES ROMANCE. IT MEANS FOREVER, BUT CAN EQUALLY EVOKE TRANSIENCE. IT IS A HERALD OF JOY, BUT ITS THORNS ARE PIERCING REMINDERS OF PAIN.

A THOUSAND GENERATIONS OF POETS HAVE DELIGHTED IN TRACING UNIVERSAL TRUTHS IN THE ROSE'S BRIEF BUT BEAUTIFUL PROGRESS FROM BUD TO DRIFTING PETALS. BECAUSE POETRY AND ROMANCE HAVE FLOURISHED WHEREVER THE ROSE HAS BLOSSOMED, IT HAS ACQUIRED LAYERS OF MEANING AND SYMBOLIC DEPTH THAT RESONATE IN THE TWENTIETH-CENTURY MIND.

NO OTHER FLOWER SURROUNDS AND CAPTURES THE SENSES LIKE THE ROSE. NO OTHER FLOWER HAS SEDUCED US SO COMPLETELY WITH ITS MYSTERIES. THIS BOOK CELEBRATES THE ROSE, WREATHED IN WORDS, GARLANDED IN PAINTINGS, AND ALWAYS CROWNED WITH PRAISE.

ROSE! THOU ART THE SWEETEST FLOWER

THAT EVER DRANK THE AMBER SHOWER;

EVEN THE GODS, WHO WALK THE SKY,

ARE AMOROUS OF THY SCENTED SIGH.

Thomas Moore (1770–1852)
Irish poet

It is perfect in every moment of its existence.

RALPH WALDO EMERSON (1803–1882)
AMERICAN WRITER

THE WILD ROSE BLOOMS, ALL SUMMER FOR HER DOWER,

NATURE'S MOST BEAUTIFUL AND PERFECT FLOWER.

George Meredith (1828–1909)
English poet and writer

Could a man make but one such rose as this, he would be thought worthy of all honour.

MARTIN LUTHER (1483–1546)
GERMAN RELIGIOUS REFORMER

I am the one rich thing that morn

    Leaves for the ardent noon

    to win;

Grasp me not, I have a thorn,

    But bend and take my

    being in.

HARRIET PRESCOTT SPOFFORD (1835–1921)
AMERICAN POET AND WRITER

James Noble

A ROSE BLOWS IN YOUR GARDEN, BUT IT CALLS YOU NOT TO SMELL IT.

John Donne (1572–1631)
English poet

eleven

he rose is more than a beautiful and popular flower, it is a great public institution.

WALTER PAGE WRIGHT (1864–1940)
ENGLISH HORTICULTURALIST

As for the roses, you could not help feeling they understood that roses are the

only flowers that impress people at garden-parties; the only flowers that

everybody is certain of knowing. Hundreds, yes, literally hundreds, had come out

in a single night; the green bushes bowed down as though they had been visited

by archangels.

KATHERINE MANSFIELD (1888–1923)
NEW ZEALAND-BORN ENGLISH WRITER

. . . and the roses were rolling over one another with that delicious superabundance of small well-tended gardens which at first sight takes away all thought from the beholder save that of beauty.

WILLIAM MORRIS (1834–1896)
ENGLISH WRITER

And I think of roses, roses,

White and red, in the wide six-

      hundred-foot greenhouses,

And my father standing astride the

      cement benches,

Lifting me high over the four-foot

      stems, the Mrs. Russells, and

      his own elaborate hybrids,

And how those flowerheads seemed to

      flow toward me, to beckon me,

      only a child, out of myself.

THEODORE ROETHKE (1908–1963)
AMERICAN POET

Perhaps few people have ever asked themselves
why they admire a rose so much more than all other flowers.
If they consider, they will find, first, that red is,
in a delicately graduated state, the loveliest of all pure colors;
and secondly, that in the rose there is no shadow,
except which is composed of color.

JOHN RUSKIN (1818–1900)
ENGLISH ARTIST AND WRITER

AND THE ROSES—THE ROSES! RISING OUT OF THE GRASS, TANGLED ROUND THE SUN-DIAL, WREATHING THE TREE TRUNKS

AND HANGING FROM THEIR BRANCHES, CLIMBING UP THE WALLS AND SPREADING OVER THEM WITH LONG GARLANDS FALLING

IN CASCADES—THEY CAME ALIVE DAY BY DAY, HOUR BY HOUR. FAIR FRESH LEAVES, AND BUDS—AND BUDS—TINY AT FIRST

BUT SWELLING AND WORKING MAGIC UNTIL THEY BURST AND UNCURLED INTO CUPS OF SCENT DELICATELY SPILLING

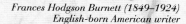

THEMSELVES OVER THEIR BRIMS AND FILLING THE GARDEN AIR.

Frances Hodgson Burnett (1849–1924)
English-born American writer

There should be beds of roses, banks of roses, bowers of roses, hedges of roses, edgings of roses, baskets of roses, vistas and alleys of roses.

REVEREND SAMUEL REYNOLDS HOLE (1819–1904)
ENGLISH CLERIC AND HORTICULTURALIST

Nature responds so beautifully

Roses are only once-wild roses, that
    were given an extra chance,

So they bloomed out and filled
    themselves with colored fulness

Out of sheer desire to be splendid, and
    more splendid.

D. H. LAWRENCE (1885–1930)
ENGLISH WRITER

WE BRING ROSES, BEAUTIFUL FRESH ROSES,

DEWY AS THE MORNING AND COLORED LIKE THE DAWN;

LITTLE TENTS OF ODOR, WHERE THE BEE REPOSES,

SWOONING IN THE SWEETNESS OF THE BED HE DREAMS UPON.

Thomas Buchanan Read (1822–1872)
American poet and painter

Grandmother has a hymn-book with great silver clasps, and she often reads in that book; in the middle of the book lies a rose, quite flat and dry; it is not as pretty as the roses she has standing in the glass; and yet she smiles at it most pleasantly of all, and tears even come into her eyes. I wonder why Grandmother looks at the withered flower in the old book that way?

HANS CHRISTIAN ANDERSEN (1805–1875)
DANISH WRITER

There's a rose looking in at the window,
  In every condition of life—
In days of content and enjoyment,
  In hours with bitterness rife.

Where'er there's the smile of a woman,
  As bright as a beam from above,
'Tis the rose looking in at the window,
  And filling the dwelling with love.

PAUL MASON JAMES (1780–1854)
ENGLISH POET

WHEN LOVE FIRST CAME TO EARTH,
  THE SPRING
SPREAD ROSE-BEDS TO RECEIVE HIM. . . .

Thomas Campbell (1777–1844)
Scottish poet

My love is like a red red rose

    That's newly sprung in June:

My love is like the melody

    That's sweetly played in tune.

ROBERT BURNS (1759–1796)
SCOTTISH POET

James Noble

The red rose whispers of passion,

And the white rose breathes of love;

O, the red rose is a falcon,

And the white rose is a dove.

But I send you a cream-white rosebud

With a flush on its petal tips;

For the love that is present and sweetest

Has a kiss of desire on the lips.

JOHN BOYLE O'REILLY (1844–1890)
IRISH-BORN AMERICAN POET AND JOURNALIST

Read in these roses the sad story

Of my hard fate and your own glory.

In the white you may discover

The paleness of a fainting lover;

In the red flames still feeding

On my heart, with fresh wounds bleeding.

THOMAS CAREW (1595–1640)
ENGLISH POET

The rose was awake all night for

your sake,

Knowing your promise to me,

The lilies and roses were

all awake,

They sighed for the dawn

and thee.

ALFRED, LORD TENNYSON (1809–1892)
ENGLISH POET

Straight go the white petals to the heart.

RICHARD JEFFERIES (1848–1887)
ENGLISH NATURALIST AND WRITER

And when I asked the like of Love
    You snatched a damask bud,

And oped it to the dainty core
    Still glowing to the last:
It was the time of roses,
    We plucked them as we
        passed.

THOMAS HOOD (1799–1845)
ENGLISH POET

. . . THE SCENT OF THE ROSE IS ENOUGH TO IMBUE A WOMAN WITH WORDLESS, SIBYLLINE POETRY, AS IF SHE WERE YOUNGER BY TEN CENTURIES.

Colette [Sidonie-Gabrielle] (1873–1954)
French writer

Change in a trice
The lilies and languors of virtue
For the raptures and roses of vice.

ALGERNON SWINBURNE (1837–1909)
ENGLISH POET

My longing drew
Me towards the rose-bush
    and then flew
Through all my soul its
    savor sweet,
Which set my heart and pulse
    abeat
Like fire.

GUILLAUME DE LORRIS
13TH-CENTURY FRENCH WRITER

"One red rose is all I want," cried the Nightingale, "only one red rose! Is there no way by which I can get it?"

"There is a way," answered the Tree; "but it is so terrible that I dare not tell it to you."

"Tell it to me," said the Nightingale, "I am not afraid."

"If you want a red rose," said the Tree, "you must build it out of music by moonlight, and stain it with your own heart's-blood. You must sing to me with your breast against a thorn. All night long you must sing to me, and the thorn must pierce your heart, and your life-blood must flow into my veins, and become mine."

OSCAR WILDE (1854–1900)
IRISH POET AND PLAYWRIGHT

A lovely being, scarcely formed

    or moulded,

A rose with all its sweetest leaves

    yet folded.

GEORGE GORDON, LORD BYRON (1789–1824)
ENGLISH POET

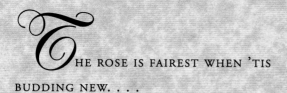

THE ROSE IS FAIREST WHEN 'TIS BUDDING NEW. . . .

Sir Walter Scott (1771–1832)
Scottish historian and writer

And on new rose-buds the new sun shall smile. . . .

WILLIAM MORRIS (1834–1896)
ENGLISH WRITER

LADY, WHEN I BEHOLD THE ROSES SPROUTING,

WHICH CLAD IN DAMASK MANTLES DECK THE ARBOURS

AND THEN BEHOLD YOUR LIPS WHERE SWEET LOVE HARBOURS

MY EYES PRESENT ME WITH A DOUBLE DOUBTING.

FOR VIEWING BOTH ALIKE, HARDLY MY MIND SUPPOSES

WHETHER THE ROSES BE YOUR LIPS OR YOUR LIPS THE ROSES.

John Wilbye (1574–1638)
English madrigal writer and musician

Rosy is the West,

Rosy is the South,

Roses are her cheeks,

And a rose her mouth.

ALFRED, LORD TENNYSON (1809–1892)
ENGLISH POET

YOUR IMAGE. . . . BLOSSOMS A ROSE IN THE DEEPS OF MY HEART.

William Butler Yeats (1865–1939)
Irish poet and playwright

THEIR LIPS WERE FOUR RED ROSES ON

A STALK,

WHICH IN THEIR SUMMER BEAUTY

KISS'D EACH OTHER.

William Shakespeare (1564–1616)
English poet and playwright

Would you appoint some flower

    to reign

In matchless beauty on the plain

The Rose (Mankind will all agree)

The Rose, the Queen of Flowers

    should be, . . .

SAPPHO (C. 610–580 B.C.)
GREEK POET

your slightest look easily will unclose me

though i have closed myself as fingers,

you open always petal by petal myself as Spring opens

(touching skilfully,mysteriously)her first rose

e. e. cummings (1894–1962)
American poet

AND THE ROSE LIKE A NYMPH TO THE

    BATH ADDREST,

WHICH UNVEILED THE DEPTH OF THE

    GLOWING BREAST,

TILL, FOLD AFTER FOLD, TO THE

    FAINTING AIR

THE SOUL OF HER BEAUTY AND LOVE

    LAY BARE.

Percy Bysshe Shelley (1792–1822)
English poet

She wore a wreath of
roses,
The night that first we
met. . . .

THOMAS HAYNES BAYLY (1797–1839)
ENGLISH POET

Alas, that Spring should vanish

with the Rose!

That Youth's sweet-scented

Manuscript should close!

EDWARD FITZGERALD (1809–1883)
ENGLISH POET

Gather ye rosebuds while ye may,

Old Time is still a-flying:

And this same flower that smiles today

Tomorrow will be dying.

ROBERT HERRICK (1591–1674)
ENGLISH POET

THE MAN WHO INVENTED THE PLASTIC ROSE

IS DEAD. BEHOLD HIS MARK:

HIS UNDYING FLAWLESS BLOSSOMS NEVER CLOSE

BUT GUARD HIS GRAVE UNBENDING THROUGH THE DARK.

HE UNDERSTOOD NEITHER BEAUTY NOR FLOWERS,

WHICH CATCH OUR HEARTS IN NETS AS SOFT AS SKY

AND BIND US WITH A THREAD OF FRAGILE HOURS:

FLOWERS ARE BEAUTIFUL BECAUSE THEY DIE.

Peter Meinke, b. 1932
American poet

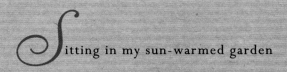

itting in my sun-warmed garden

eyes closed I hear

very soft

a melancholy song

It is the dying roses

lamenting

in pale pink voices

their fading lives. . . .

MICHAEL BULLOCK, B. 1918
ENGLISH-BORN CANADIAN POET

'*Tis the last rose of summer*
Left blooming alone;
All her lovely companions
Are faded and gone.

THOMAS MOORE (1779–1852)
IRISH POET

THE SUN WENT SLEEPILY DOWN IN THE WEST;

AND THE ROSES CRIED, AS THEY SAW HIM GO:

"OH, STAY WITH US, SUN, FOR

we love you best."

SO THERE STAYED A WHILE WITH THE COMING NIGHT,

SWEET FLUSHES OF LIGHT THAT

WOULD SOFTLY PRESS

A KISS ON THE LIPS OF THOSE ROSES WHITE,

TILL THEIR LEAVES BLUSHED

RED AT THE SWEET CARESS.

Edric Vredenburg, b. 1860
English editor and writer

ILLUSTRATION ACKNOWLEDGMENTS

COVER: *The Last Roses of Summer*, James Noble

TITLE PAGE: *Crimson Quintet*, James Noble

p. 7: *Flower Arrangement*, Albert Williams (N. E. Middleton)

p. 8 [detail]: *June Bouquet*, Vernon Ward

p. 10–11: *Papa Meilland Roses*, James Noble

p. 12: *A Summer Bouquet*, John Strevens

p. 14–15 [detail]: *Flowering Summer*, Anna Zinkeisen

p. 16: *The Last Roses of Summer*, James Noble

p. 19 [detail]: *Wings Upon a Rose*, Vernon Ward

p. 20-21: *Rosa Alba Maxima*, Leslie Greenwood

p. 23: *Strawberry Tea*, Catherine Tyler (Montague Ward, Wadhurst, Sussex)

p. 24: *Roses are Red*, James Noble

p. 27: *Sleepy*, Eva Hollyer (Fine Art Photographic Library Limited)

p. 28 [detail]: *In the Rose Garden*, Thomas James Lloyd (Fine Art Photographic Library Limited)

p. 30: *Scarlet Roses in a Goblet*, James Noble

p. 32: *A Christmas Greeting*, Charles Trevor Garland (Fine Art Photographic Library Limited)

p. 35 [detail]: *Roses and Pansies*, Albert Williams (N. E. Middleton)

p. 36 [detail]: *Pink Roses*, Chris Hill (N. E. Middleton)

p. 38: *Red Devil Roses in a Green Glass Vase*, James Noble

p. 41 [detail]: *The Bridesmaid*, John Phillip (Tunbridge Wells Museum and Art Gallery)

p. 43: *Roses*, Ethel Buckingham (Norfolk Museums Service (Norwich Castle Museum))

p. 45: *Summer Flowers*, Anna Zinkeisen

p. 46: *Camphill Glory*, John Lancaster